W9-ATA-197

George W. Bush

The War on Terrorism

By Jill C. Wheeler

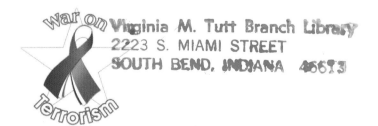

Visit us at
www.abdopub.com

Published by ABDO & Daughters, an imprint of ABDO Publishing Company, 4940 Viking Drive, Suite 622, Edina, Minnesota 55435. Copyright ©2002 by Abdo Consulting Group, Inc. International copyrights reserved in all countries. No part of this book may be reproduced in any form without written permission from the publisher.

Printed in the United States.

Edited by Paul Joseph
Graphic Design: John Hamilton
Cover Design: Mighty Media
Photos: AP/Photo, FEMA, SpaceImaging.com
Illustrations: John Hamilton

Library of Congress Cataloging-in-Publication Data

Wheeler, Jill C., 1964-
  George W. Bush / Jill C. Wheeler.
    p. cm. — (War on terrorism)
  Includes index.
  ISBN 1-57765-662-8
  1. Bush, George W. (George Walker), 1946—Juvenile literature. 2. Presidents—United States—Biography—Juvenile literature. 3. September 11 Terrorist Attacks, 2001—Juvenile literature. I. Title. II. Series.

E903.W47 2002
973.928'092—dc21
[B]

2001055242

Table of Contents

A New Agenda 5

Commander In Chief 9

Political Heritage 13

Moving Up In Midland 16

In His Father's Footsteps 19

In The Guard 25

The Oil Business 28

Growing Up 31

To The White House 35

A Warning To Terrorists 38

Rallying A Troubled World 41

Where On The Web? 45

Timeline 46

Glossary 47

Index 48

Chilling News

White House Chief of Staff Andy Card tells President Bush that a plane has crashed into New York's World Trade Center. The president was visiting Emma E. Booker Elementary School in Sarasota, Florida, September 11, 2001, when the terrorist attacks occurred.

A New Agenda

SOME PEOPLE MAY HAVE THOUGHT GEORGE W. Bush sounded like a broken record. During his presidential campaign, he talked repeatedly about the same issues. One of them was reforming education. He had helped do that in Texas as governor. If elected president of the United States, he said he would help students throughout the country get a better education.

On September 11, 2001, he was at it again. That morning, Bush was visiting Emma E. Booker Elementary School in Sarasota, Florida. When he arrived at the school, White House Chief of Staff Andy Card took him aside. He told him a plane had crashed into the World Trade Center in New York City. He also said United States National Security Adviser Condoleezza Rice wanted to talk to him.

After talking briefly with Rice, Bush was introduced to a classroom of excited second graders. He smiled and listened as the students recited their reading drills for him. Afterwards, he got ready to pose for pictures with the students and the school staff. Just then, Card approached him again and whispered in his ear.

United Airlines Flight 175 moments before crashing into the South Tower of the World Trade Center.

The students watched the president's face become tense and serious. When Card left, President Bush did his best to talk to the students again. "Really good readers," he said. "These must be sixth graders!" The children laughed. They may also have sensed that his thoughts clearly were elsewhere. Chief of Staff Card had told the president that a second plane had just crashed into the World Trade Center. Clearly, it was not an accident.

The president gave a brief address after his visit to the school. Local politicians, school staff, and students all had gathered. Bush spoke only briefly, his face tense and concerned.

"This is a difficult time for America," he said. He announced that the nation had suffered a terrorist attack. Then he called for an investigation to find the people responsible for the attack. Following the short address, he called Vice President Dick Cheney. He also spoke with Federal Bureau of Investigation (FBI) officials in Washington, D.C. When he hung up the phone, he turned to his staff. "We're at war," he said. Within hours, his agenda had changed. Education reform would have to wait. Now was the time for justice.

Boarding Air Force One

President Bush waves as he boards Air Force One September 11, 2001, at Sarasota-Bradenton International Airport.

President George W. Bush

Shortly after learning of the terrorist attacks, President Bush was whisked away aboard Air Force One.

Commander In Chief

WHEN THE PRESIDENT OF THE UNITED States travels, he takes a special plane called Air Force One. Air Force One is specially designed so the president can work while on board. It also is designed to be as safe as possible. Despite that, many of the president's assistants were concerned about his safety on September 11. The officials sent bomb-sniffing dogs to double-check the plane before President Bush boarded it in Florida.

President Bush told his staff members he wanted to immediately return to Washington, D.C. The Secret Service officers assigned to protect him disagreed. By this time, a third hijacked plane had crashed into the Pentagon. The Secret Service agents also had heard that there might be still more targets that day. The White House or even Air Force One might be one of those targets. While the Federal Aviation Administration (FAA) had halted all air traffic, some planes still were in the air. Those planes also would be grounded once they reached their destination. Until then, the agents urged Bush to avoid returning to Washington.

President Bush agreed reluctantly. He ordered U.S. military forces to their highest level of alert status. Then, just before 10 A.M., he boarded Air Force One and left Florida. The plane was bound for Barksdale Air Force Base in Louisiana. Bush wanted to go somewhere where he could address the nation. Vice President Cheney had suggested the president go to a secure military base instead of Washington, D.C. Barksdale was not where Bush wanted to be. However, he realized it would be foolish to risk flying straight into another attack.

The president made many phone calls during the two-hour flight to Barksdale. "That's what we're paid for, boys," he told his aides. "We're gonna take care of this. We're going to find out who did this. They're not going to like me as president."

By the time Bush arrived, Americans had not heard from their president in three hours. Many were wondering where he was. Why was he not rallying a shocked nation?

Those who knew Bush well understood. He works best away from the glare of cameras and publicity. He is most effective behind the scenes, negotiating and making deals. While Americans didn't see him, he was very busy the morning of September 11 being the commander in chief. He was in almost constant contact with his senior officials. They were working to prevent further attacks. They also were planning how to find out who had committed the terrorist acts.

After arriving at Barksdale, Bush made his public statement. He reassured Americans that he had ordered security measures to stop further attacks. He asked for prayers for those killed or wounded in the attacks. Finally, he promised justice. "Make no mistake," he told the world. "The United States will hunt down and punish those responsible for these cowardly acts... We will show the world that we will pass this test."

America Strikes Back

While flying to a secure area aboard Air Force One, President Bush keeps in touch with his staff and Congressional leaders.

Day of Prayer

Former President George H. W. Bush, center, reaches over to his son, President George W. Bush, during a church service September 14, 2001. To his father's left is the president's mother, Barbara Bush. To her left is former President Bill Clinton.

Political Heritage

THE TEST POSED TO THE U.S. ALSO WAS THE first major test for George W. Bush. He had been president for less than eight months when the September 11 attacks occurred. Both before and after his election, he had many critics. His critics said he didn't have the experience he needed to lead. They guessed had it not been for his background, he never would have been elected.

George W. Bush comes from a family with a long history in politics. He was born in New Haven, Connecticut, on July 6, 1946. His parents were George Herbert Walker Bush and Barbara Pierce Bush. His father would go on to become the 41st president of the United States. George W.'s grandfather, Prescott Bush, was a U.S. senator. Tall and stern, Prescott was a powerful and important figure in the Bush family. Young George W. quickly learned to mind his manners around his grandfather.

At the time of George W.'s birth, his father, George H. W., was still in school at Yale University. He was a little older than many of the students because he had served in World War II before college. George H. W. was a navy fighter pilot in the war. He flew many missions and became a hero after he was shot down at sea and rescued by a submarine.

In January 1945, George H. W. married Barbara Pierce. The two had met at a dance in 1941. Barbara was the daughter of a successful publisher. She also was a descendent of the 14ᵗʰ U.S. president, Franklin Pierce. Like her husband, she had grown up in a wealthy and privileged family and had attended only the best schools.

The newlyweds made their home in New Haven while George H. W. finished his studies at Yale. Shortly after George W.'s birth, Prescott Bush offered his son a job with the family's oil company. There was only one catch—the job was in Odessa, Texas. George H. W. accepted. The day after graduating from Yale in 1948, he headed west. Barbara and two-year-old George W. joined him one week later.

West Texas looked nothing like Connecticut. It was flat and dusty, with virtually no trees. Tumbleweeds often blew down the streets. Sometimes the air smelled of the nearby oil refineries. The Bush family lived in a two-room apartment and shared a bathroom with another family. It was very different from what the Bushes were used to. For George W., it was heaven. There was plenty of room for a young boy to play. He also loved to go out to the oil fields with his father.

The following year, the Bushes had a daughter, Pauline Robinson. They called her Robin. In 1950, the Bush family moved to Midland, Texas. Midland and Odessa sometimes are called sister cities. They are next to one another, yet in the 1950s they were very different. Odessa was where most of the blue-collar oil workers lived. Midland was where the oil company executives lived.

The Bush family bought a new two-bedroom home on a dirt road in a development called Easter Egg Row. People called it that because the houses all looked alike except for their color.

George W. made many new friends along Easter Egg Row. Most of them had parents in the oil business, too. One of George W.'s favorite things to do was to put on his cowboy hat and boots and play with his friends. In the summer, the heat in West Texas became almost unbearable. During that time, the Bushes packed up and went to Maine. The Bush family had an estate there, and it was much cooler than in Texas.

The Dynasty

The Bush family in 1948, left to right: mother Barbara, George W., father George, and grandparents Dorothy and Prescott Bush.

Moving Up In Midland

N 1952, THE BUSHES MOVED TO A LARGER HOME IN Midland. This one was on a paved street. George H. W. now owned his own oil company, and it was doing well. George W. spent his time riding bikes, playing with friends, and going to Sam Houston Elementary School. In February 1953, a new brother joined George W. and Robin. His name was John Ellis Bush. The family called him Jeb. The Bush family was delighted to welcome Jeb. Yet their happiness soon faded. Just weeks after Jeb's birth, doctors found a problem with Robin. They said she was very sick with leukemia. Robin died in October 1953. She was just three years old.

Robin's death was hard on everyone in the family. George W. was sad for a long time. His mother, Barbara, didn't smile as much anymore. Her beautiful auburn hair started to turn gray though she was only 28 years old. George W. took to spending more time with his mother to try to cheer her up.

With many of the fathers in the neighborhood busy in the oil business, the mothers and children spent a lot of time together. The Bush home became one of their favorite gathering places. Many of the other mothers enjoyed spending time with Barbara. George also was popular among the other children. He was outgoing and talkative, and he adored sports.

When George W. and his father had time together, they loved to play ball or talk baseball. In fact, the whole Bush family enjoyed baseball. George W. would memorize the starting lineup of his favorite teams.

In 1955, the Bush family moved to an even larger house in Midland. This one had a swimming pool. The Bush family now included another son, Neil. The following year, a fourth son was born. They named him Marvin, after Barbara's father.

Barbara had her hands full with four boys. George W. often fought with Jeb, and he got into his share of problems at school. In third grade, he threw a football through the window. The following year, he was sent to the principal for imitating Elvis Presley in class.

Barbara wouldn't allow any misbehavior at home. Once George W. made the mistake of saying something insulting about African Americans. Immediately, Barbara dragged him to the bathroom and washed his mouth out with soap. The Bush family was loving but stern. The children learned it was important to follow rules. They also learned that it was important to be loyal to friends and family. Once again, the skill would serve George W. the politician well.

George W. Bush, center, poses with his father George Bush and mother Barbara Bush during the summer of 1955.

Father and Son

President George W. Bush escorts his father, former President George H. W. Bush, to a church service near the family's estate at Kennebunkport, Maine.

In His Father's Footsteps

OUNG GEORGE W. LOVED BASEBALL. WHEN he was 10, he made the Midland Little League team. From that point on, he spent every spare minute playing baseball. His father had been a baseball star at Yale. George W. wanted to excel as well. He even dreamed of playing in the major leagues.

George W.'s baseball talent was just average. He made up for that with persistence and hard work. He played catcher so he could be involved in as many plays as possible.

In the fall of 1958, George W. attended San Jacinto Junior High in Midland. He played football there and even was elected class president. However, he had to leave after just one year. His father's oil business had moved most operations from West Texas to offshore. Now it was more convenient for the family to live in Houston, Texas. Shortly after George W. and his three brothers finished school and moved, they found themselves with a new little sister. Her name was Dorothy Walker Bush.

In Houston, the Bush family had an even larger home. This one had a swimming pool *and* a private baseball field. George W. began attending classes at Kincaid School. It was one of the most exclusive private schools in all of Texas. George W.'s outgoing manner and ability to remember people's names won him many new friends. Once again, he became a class officer.

Though Kincaid was a good school, his parents had other things in mind for George W. It was a tradition for the young men in the Bush family to attend Phillips Academy, a prep school in Andover, Massachusetts. George H. W. had gone there, as had Prescott Bush. Now the family expected George W. to go. He applied, and in the fall of 1961, 15-year-old George W. left Texas for New England.

Winters in Andover were cold and damp, and Phillips had no girls and many strict rules. In class, George W. had to work harder than ever. He worried about flunking his classes and disgracing his family. Yet he learned to study harder, and he quickly made friends. He had an ability to get people to laugh with his quick remarks. He was a lot like his mother in that way. It wasn't long before his friends gave him a nickname. It was Lip.

George W. learned to like Andover. He played basketball and baseball and joined the Spanish Club. Friends remember him as one of the friendliest students at the school. He became a cheerleader to pump up school spirit at games. And he kept in close touch with the Bush family back in Houston. Things were becoming even more interesting back home. George W. knew his father believed that people with wealth and ability had a duty to serve in public office. He had learned that from his father, Prescott. Now, George H. W. was going to put that belief into action. In September 1963, George H. W. announced he was going to run for a seat in the U.S. Senate.

School Spirit

George W. Bush was the head cheerleader at Phillips Academy in 1964.

George W. Bush never had been very interested in politics. He admitted he didn't like to study political issues. After four years at Andover, George W. was accepted at Yale University. But before starting at Yale, he took the summer off to help with his father's Senate campaign. He wasn't that interested in politics but he did want to help his father become a senator.

George W. was a natural at campaigning. He had a special ability to remember people's names and make friends with them. He and Barbara helped George H. W. campaign against his much more popular opponent. Despite their efforts, he lost the election. The following year, George H. W. announced he was going to try again—this time for a seat in the U.S. House of Representatives. George W. was proud of his father for his determination. "This is what you do," he told a friend. "You bounce back."

Yale Man

George W. Bush at Yale University in New Haven, Connecticut.

At Yale, George W. continued to avoid politics. Instead, he joined a fraternity that focused on sports and parties. It was a perfect fit for the very social George W. He loved anything that involved being around other people. Eventually, he was elected president of the fraternity. He also was invited to join Skull and Bones. Skull and Bones was among the most elite of Yale's secret societies. His father had been a member, too.

During the first summer at Yale, George W. had worked for his father on an offshore oil rig. He knew he never wanted to do that hot, back-breaking work again. His second summer, he worked in a department store. His people skills made him a successful salesperson. He also helped with his father's campaign that summer. This time their hard work paid off. George H. W. won his race that November in 1966.

George W. was proud to have his father in Washington, D.C. That didn't stop him from getting into his share of mischief, however. Once, he and some friends stole a Christmas wreath for their fraternity house. Another time, he and some other students tore down the goalposts after a Yale-Princeton game. Both times he had skirmishes with the police.

George W. wasn't always perfectly behaved. Yet he never challenged the establishment of which his family was a part. He might rebel in small ways. He would never rebel in a big way that would bring shame to his family. Nor would he ever turn his back on his family's values.

Air Guard

Air Guard

George W. Bush as a pilot in the Texas Air National Guard.

In The Guard

**O**N SEPTEMBER 12, 2001, PRESIDENT GEORGE W. Bush declared that the attack on America had been "an act of war." As he vowed to fight terrorism, he also warned Americans. The war on terrorism, he said, would be unlike any other war America had fought.

Likewise, the Vietnam War was unlike any war America had ever fought up to that time. And unlike other wars, it did not have the broad support of the American people. While George H. W. Bush had gone off to World War II with cheers and flags, the soldiers who served in Vietnam often were greeted with hostility. For George W. and others in his Yale class, Vietnam was a place none of them wanted to go.

Many young men avoided serving in Vietnam by going to college. When college was over, they had to find something else. George W. did not want to dodge military service completely after Yale. However, he did not want to go to Vietnam. Thanks to his family's influence, he was able to get one of two pilot slots in the Texas Air National Guard. There he could fulfill his military service safely.

Many people have criticized George W. for not serving in Vietnam. The truth is, only a handful of the sons of congressmen ever did. Two-hundred-thirty-four sons of senators and congressmen came of age during Vietnam. Only 28 of them actually went to Vietnam.

In the Texas Air National Guard, George W. learned how to fly airplanes. He received his pilot's wings in December 1969. He loved to fly, and he did it well. He also was popular among the other guardsmen.

Back in the Bush home in Houston, George H. W. had decided to leave the U.S. House of Representatives after two terms. He wanted to seek a Senate seat again. As before, George W. jumped in to help with the campaign. He often appeared with his father in his National Guard flight jacket. When not campaigning, he enjoyed attending parties at the Houston apartment he now called home.

George H. W. lost his senate race in November 1970. Fortunately, then-President Richard Nixon offered him a job as U.S. ambassador to the United Nations. George H. W. and Barbara moved to New York City. George W. remained in Houston. He did his National Guard time on weekends. He also wondered what he should do with the rest of his life. He had applied to and been rejected by the University of Texas law school. He also had tried a nine-to-five job with an agribusiness company. He hated that job and quit after less than a year.

George W. began to think about going into politics himself. His father had a better idea, however. He suggested his son get a job working on a friend's political campaign in Alabama. He thought the job would be good experience for his son. George W. worked on the campaign as his father had suggested. It *was* a good experience for him, even though his candidate lost.

After the election, George W. took a job with a program that helped disadvantaged kids in inner-city Houston. The program also involved professional athletes, who served as mentors to the kids. It was a perfect job for George W. He could use his people skills and connections to raise money for the program. He also got to spend time with children. George W. loved working with kids.

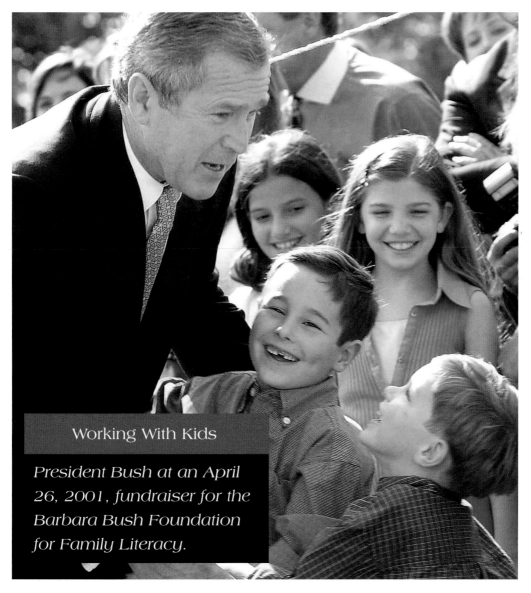

Working With Kids

President Bush at an April 26, 2001, fundraiser for the Barbara Bush Foundation for Family Literacy.

The Oil Business

T AGE 26, GEORGE W. STILL WAS NOT SURE if politics was where he wanted to be. He decided to attend Harvard Business School instead. If he didn't go into politics, he likely would be asked to help with the family oil business. A Harvard business education would be useful for that.

George W. graduated from Harvard in spring 1975. By then, he had heard there was a new oil boom in Texas. He decided to go into the oil business himself. He moved back to Midland and was delighted to get together with many of his old friends.

In August 1977, one of those friends invited him to a party. He introduced George W. to a young elementary school librarian named Laura Welch. Quiet, shy, and beautiful, Laura didn't enjoy politics. She knew George W. was from a very wealthy and political family. In spite of this, she found she truly enjoyed his company. The two began to date, and it wasn't long before George W. told his family he had met someone special.

Life-of-the-party George W. had dated many women. He'd even been engaged once during college. But this woman was different—and very different from George W. One Texas journalist commented that George W. "was exactly the kind of guy librarians would tell to shut up in the library."

George W. and Laura were married on November 5, 1977, in Midland. They didn't have time for a honeymoon, however. George W. was knee-deep in a political campaign again. This time, it was his own campaign for the U.S. House of Representatives. He lost the race.

George H. W. Bush hadn't won any elections since his loss in 1970, either. He had, however, still been active in politics. Along with his post with the United Nations, he had served as unofficial ambassador to China. He also worked briefly as director of the U.S. Central Intelligence Agency (CIA). In 1980, he lost the Republican presidential nomination to Ronald Reagan. Reagan then invited George H. W. to be his vice president.

The Campaign Trail

George W. Bush with his wife, Laura, campaigning for Congress in 1978.

A Changed Man

During the early 1980s, and despite business setbacks, George W. Bush refocused his life to become a better husband and father.

Growing Up

GEORGE W. WAS PROUD TO STAND AT HIS father's side when he was sworn in as vice president of the United States in January 1981. He was even more proud on November 25, 1981, when Laura gave birth to twin daughters Jenna and Barbara.

George W. enjoyed being a father. He also enjoyed being a part of the Midland community. He jogged every day regardless of the heat. He knew and talked with virtually everyone when he walked into the local diner for lunch. He even laughed when the local country club created a George W. Bush Award for the worst-dressed golfer.

If there was a dark spot in George W.'s life, it was his oil business. West Texas wasn't a good place to be in the oil business in the 1980s. George W. and his investors lost millions of dollars before another company bought his company. Some people guessed George W. only was able to sell his company because his father was vice president.

Around the same time, George made the decision to quit drinking alcohol. All his life he had loved parties and loved drinking. He now realized his drinking had a negative side. When he drank, he often lost his temper or said things he later regretted. "I felt different," George said of his decision to quit drinking. "I had more time to read. I had more energy. I became a better listener and not such an incessant talker."

His timing couldn't have been better. By 1988, his father was running for president of the United States. George W. didn't dare say or do anything that might hurt his father's campaign. Nor could he afford to have his father's critics pointing to George W.'s drinking problem. When it came to campaigns, George W. completely understood the need to put on the best possible appearance.

Proud Father

George W. Bush in 1981 with his newborn twin daughters, Jenna and Barbara.

George H. W. Bush was elected president in 1988. At the end of that year, George W. moved his family to Dallas, Texas. He had a new job working with investors to buy the Texas Rangers baseball team. It was a dream job for George W. He knew how to raise money, and he adored baseball. The job also gave him a lot of visibility among Texans. In the back of his mind, he began planning a run for governor of Texas.

George W. knew that in politics, timing was everything. He also knew 1990 would not be the year. For starters, his father was president. Two Bushes would be simply too confusing. So he decided to wait. When his father lost his re-election bid in 1992 to Bill Clinton, George W. began to focus on his plans. In the fall of 1993, he announced his bid for governor of Texas.

At the time, the governor of Texas was Democrat Ann Richards. Richards was popular and effective. George W. and his team knew it would be a difficult campaign. Even Barbara Bush told him, "You can't win." Yet George W. had made up his mind. He knew the issues he wanted to stress. He would talk about fighting crime, improving education, and reforming welfare and the legal system.

Throughout the campaign, George W. stuck to his topics. He refused to say bad things about Ann Richards. Miraculously, he kept his temper the entire time. On Election Day, he won by the largest margin in Texas in 20 years. Clearly, George W. had learned many lessons from his family about campaigning. In January 1995, he was sworn in as governor of Texas.

Candidate Bush

George W. Bush on the 2000 presidential campaign trail.

To The White House

GOVERNOR GEORGE W. BUSH RAN THE STATE of Texas much like he'd run the rest of his life. He knew everyone and what they did. Rather than trying to learn everything about an issue, he asked people who already knew. He made friends with powerful people. They were the people in the starting lineup of politics. He used his warmth and charm to get people to agree so things could happen.

Ann Richards had set in motion many positive changes in the educational system in Texas. Governor Bush continued down that path. As a firm believer in business, Governor Bush worked to make it harder for people to sue businesses in court. Conservative voters and leaders were glad to see him increase penalties for crimes and force people on welfare to get jobs. Governor Bush had done what he said he would do when campaigning. He easily won re-election in 1998. That made him the first governor in Texas history to serve two terms.

George W. Bush enjoyed being governor of Texas. However, he had his eye on being president of the United States. And he knew the timing was 2000 or never. He felt he had gifts that would help the nation. He had a talent to work with people to get things done, even if those people disagreed.

His campaign for president was tough and long. He had many advantages, however. People knew his name. More importantly, he could easily raise the millions of dollars necessary to run a successful campaign. In just his first month of fund-raising he landed $7.5 million. People gave money because they liked George W. Bush, and he seemed to be enthusiastic about them as well.

George W. Bush's toughest opponents were Arizona Senator John McCain and Vice President Al Gore. Bush beat McCain in the Republican primaries. Now it was Bush against Gore. Gore accused Bush of not having enough experience in politics. Bush turned that into an advantage. Perhaps more importantly, Al Gore appeared to people as a cold intellectual. Bush seemed to voters to be the warm, friendly guy next door. In debates, Gore showed superior knowledge of the issues, but he also appeared cold. Bush only discussed the messages he had practiced, and he didn't lose his temper. He used only simple messages. He promised to solve problems and bring people together.

Bush and Gore were neck and neck at the polls on Election Day. The race pivoted on the results in Florida. At first, people thought Gore had won Florida. Then, it was announced Bush had won Florida. Ballot recounts followed. When Florida officials refused to allow the recounts to continue, the Gore campaign went to court. The issue eventually went all the way to the United States Supreme Court. Five weeks and many court decisions later, George W. Bush was declared the winner.

Some people still believe that Al Gore actually had more votes in Florida. Some Democratic voters in Florida talked about having problems casting their ballots. In addition, George W. Bush's brother, Jeb, was governor of Florida at the time. The people who supported Gore wondered if Jeb Bush had helped fix the election so his brother would win.

The close election and rumors of cheating followed Bush to Washington, D.C. When he was sworn in as president in January 2001, he knew he had a tough job ahead. Somehow, he had to pull a splintered nation back together. Few people would have guessed the answer to that problem would come in the form of a terrorist attack.

Election Controversy

Protesters face off outside the United States Supreme Court in Washington, D.C.

A Warning To Terrorists

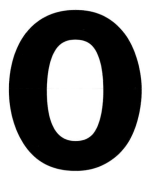

ON SEPTEMBER 11, 2001, PRESIDENT BUSH was on the phone with many loyal friends and advisers. After leaving Barksdale Air Force Base aboard Air Force One, he flew to Offut Air Force Base near Omaha, Nebraska. Offut is home to the Strategic Air Command center. It is one of the most secure military bases in the world. At Offut, the president conferred with Vice President Cheney and National Security Advisor Rice. They and other leaders now were operating out of a special bunker on the White House grounds. They worked to sort out what the attacks meant and what else might be happening.

President Bush also called his wife, Laura, and his father, former President George H. W. Bush. Then he talked to New York City Mayor Rudolph Giuliani and New York Governor George Pataki. The three men discussed emergency responses to help the victims and rescuers in New York City.

Finally, the president grew too impatient. "I want to go back to Washington as soon as possible—now," he snapped to his aides. "I don't want any tinhorn dictator terrorist holding me outside Washington. The American people want to see their president, and they want to see him in Washington."

At 4:30 p.m., Air Force One left Offut for Washington, D.C., with F-16 fighter jets escorting it. When Air Force One landed at Andrews Air Force Base in Maryland, President Bush was transferred to Marine One. The helicopter landed on the White House grounds just before 7:00 P.M. The scene was far different from when he left. Now armed guards were at every corner. They even patrolled the park across the street. At 8:30 P.M., he addressed a shocked and grieving nation from the Oval Office.

"Thousands of lives were suddenly ended by evil, despicable acts of terror," Bush said. "These acts shattered steel, but they cannot dent the steel of American resolve." He said government functions would continue without interruption despite the attacks. He also warned that the U.S. would not tolerate those who helped the terrorists. Anyone helping terrorists would be treated the same as the terrorists themselves.

The words were not surprising for those who knew George W. Bush. Once he made up his mind to do something, he did it.

President Bush warned terrorist groups that the United States will do whatever it takes to get justice for the attacks of September 11, 2001.

At Ground Zero

President Bush visits rescue and recovery workers at the site of the World Trade Center collapse in New York City.

Rallying A Troubled World

Y THE END OF THE FIRST WEEK AFTER THE attacks, President George W. Bush had taken charge. On Wednesday morning he met with senior national security advisers. The advisers had begun to piece together the events of the previous day. They outlined what they believed had happened. They told him their initial investigations pointed toward the al-Qaeda (all-KIGH-duh) network of terrorists. A man named Osama bin Laden (oh-SAH-MA bin LAH-dun) leads the al-Qaeda.

President Bush listened quietly and outlined what needed to be done. He knew he had to authorize money and manpower for the rescue efforts under way. He also had to craft a careful plan to fight terrorism. He had to find and bring to justice the people responsible for so many deaths.

Later that day, the president met with members of Congress. He also spoke with many foreign leaders. The leaders told Bush how sorry they were that the attacks had happened. Wednesday evening, Bush visited the Pentagon and thanked rescue workers for their efforts. "Coming here makes me sad, on the one hand," he said. "It also makes me angry." On Thursday, September 13, President Bush talked again with Mayor Giuliani and Governor Pataki. He promised them the government would help them rebuild.

President Bush declared Friday, September 14, a national day of prayer and remembrance. That morning, he spoke at a special memorial service at the Washington National Cathedral. He then flew to New York City to visit the rubble of the World Trade Center. There, rescue workers cheered as he told them, "I can hear you. The rest of the world hears you. And the people who knocked these buildings down will hear all of us soon."

Target: Bin Laden

A photo of Osama bin Laden taken sometime in 1998.

President George W. Bush holds up the police shield of New York Police Officer George Howard, who died trying to save others in the World Trade Center.

President Bush's popularity skyrocketed. The man who once had been called Big Man on Campus, was now Big Man on the Capitol. In a poll conducted by *Newsweek* just after the September 11 attacks, 82 percent of those surveyed said they approved of how President Bush was handling the crisis. That approval rating virtually equaled the approval rating of Franklin Delano Roosevelt following the attack on Pearl Harbor. It also was higher than any marks received by any other modern president.

President Bush had incredible support. He also faced a huge task. He had to quickly mobilize a worldwide coalition against terrorism. He had to reach out to friends and former enemies for help. And he had to prepare his nation for a long war on terrorism. It would not, he told people, be quick or easy. It would involve sacrifices and inconveniences. President Bush knew that the longer the war dragged on, the less likely people were to support it. He had to begin work now to build a foundation for what appeared to be a long-term conflict.

On Thursday, September 20, President George W. Bush addressed a joint session of Congress. "Either you are with us or you are with the terrorists," he told them. He calmly assured Congress and the millions of Americans tuning in to hear him, "Justice will be done."

The address was broadcast around the world. Millions of those who watched felt it was the new president's best speech yet. In the eyes of a shaken world, George W. Bush was becoming just the leader he needed to be.

On Sunday, October 7, President Bush began the war on terrorism. The American military began bombing the country of Afghanistan in hopes of destroying the al-Qaeda terrorist network. President Bush has the hardest job of anyone in the world but his admirers and critics alike believe he is up to the task.

A U.S. Navy F/A-18C Hornet lands on the flight deck of the aircraft carrier USS *Carl Vinson* during Operation Enduring Freedom.

Where On The Web?

http://www.whitehouse.gov/
The official site of the White House. Includes news, photos, and a special section just for kids.

http://search.biography.com/cgi-bin/frameit.cgi?p=http%3A//
search.biography.com/print_record.pl%3Fid%3D23367
From A&E television, a Biography.com section devoted to George W. Bush.

http://www.lib.umich.edu/govdocs/usterror.html
The University of Michigan Document Center site provides web links to a wealth of information regarding the September 11 terrorism attacks.

http://www.infoplease.com/spot/
campaign2000wrapup.html
From Infoplease.com, a complete wrap-up of the 2000 election campaign.

http://www.multied.com/elections/
From History Central, a chronology of each United States presidential election.

Timeline

1946	George W. Bush born July 6 in New Haven, Connecticut.
1948	Family moves to Odessa, Texas.
1950	Family moves to Midland, Texas.
1953	Sister Robin dies.
1959	Family moves to Houston, Texas.
1961	Enters Phillips Academy in Andover, Massachusetts.
1964	Graduates from Andover; works on father's Senate campaign; enters Yale University.
1968	Graduates from Yale; joins Texas Air National Guard.
1969	Earns National Guard pilot's wings.
1970	Works on father's Senate campaign.
1973	Enters Harvard Business School.
1975	Graduates from Harvard; returns to Midland, Texas.
1977	Starts Arbusto Energy; marries Laura Welch.
1978	Runs for Congress, loses.
1981	Daughters Jenna and Barbara born; changes company name to Bush Exploration.
1984	Spectrum 7 buys Bush Exploration.
1986	Harken Energy buys Spectrum 7.
1988	Works on father's presidential campaign.
1989	Joins investment group that buys Texas Rangers.
1994	Elected governor of Texas.
1998	Re-elected governor of Texas.
2000	Elected president of United States.

Glossary

blue collar
People whose jobs involve manual labor.

bunker
A sturdy room, usually underground, that can withstand an attack.

coalition
A group of organizations or countries that agree to work together.

leukemia
A form of cancer that interferes with the body's production of healthy blood cells. It makes a body unable to protect itself against infections.

mentor
A counselor who advises someone, often about career issues.

prep school
A school that prepares students for college.

tinhorn
Someone who pretends to be more powerful than they are.

Index

A
Air Force One 9, 10, 38, 39
al-Qaeda 41, 44
Andover, MA 20, 21
Andrews Air Force Base 39
Arizona 36

B
Barksdale Air Force Base 10, 38
bin Laden, Osama 41
Bush, Barbara (daughter) 31
Bush, Barbara (mother) 13, 14, 16, 17, 22, 26, 33
Bush, Dorothy Walker 19
Bush, George Herbert Walker 13, 14, 16, 20, 22, 23, 25, 26, 29, 33, 38
Bush, Jeb 16, 17, 36, 37
Bush, Jenna 31
Bush, John Ellis 16
Bush, Laura 28, 29, 31, 38
Bush, Marvin Pierce 17
Bush, Neil Mallon 17
Bush, Pauline Robinson "Robin" 14, 16
Bush, Prescott 13, 14, 20

C
Card, Andy 5, 6
Central Intelligence Agency 29

Cheney, Dick 6, 10, 38
Clinton, Bill 33
Congress 42, 44
Connecticut 13, 14

D
Dallas, TX 33

E
Emma E. Booker Elementary School 5

F
Federal Aviation Administration 9
Federal Bureau of Investigation 6
Florida 5, 9, 10, 36

G
Giuliani, Rudolph 38, 42
Gore, Al 36, 37

H
Harvard 28
House of Representatives 22, 26, 29
Houston, TX 16, 19, 20, 26, 27

K
Kincaid School 20

L
Louisiana 10

M
Marine One 39
Maryland 39
Massachusetts 20
McCain, John 36
Midland, TX 14, 16, 17, 19, 28, 29, 31

Midland Little League 19

N
Nebraska 38
New England 20
New Haven, CT 13, 14
New York, NY 5, 26, 38, 42
Newsweek 43
Nixon, Richard 26

O
Odessa, TX 14
Offut Air Force Base 38, 39
Omaha, NE 38
Oval Office 39

P
Pataki, George 38, 42
Pearl Harbor 43
Pentagon 9, 42
Phillips Academy 20
Princeton University 23

R
Reagan, Ronald 29
Rice, Condoleezza 5, 38
Richards, Ann 33, 35
Roosevelt, Franklin Delano 43

S
Sam Houston Elementary School 16
San Jacinto Junior High 19
Sarasota, FL 5
Secret Service 9
Senate 20, 21, 26
Skull and Bones 23

Spanish Club 20
Strategic Air Command 38
Supreme Court 36

T
Texas 5, 14, 15, 19, 20, 25, 26, 28, 31, 33, 35
Texas Air National Guard 25, 26
Texas Rangers 33

U
United Nations 26, 29
University of Texas 26

V
Vietnam 25, 26
Vietnam War 25

W
Washington, D.C. 6, 9, 10, 23, 37, 38, 39, 42
White House 5, 9, 38, 39
World Trade Center 5, 6, 42
World War II 13, 25

Y
Yale University 13, 14, 19, 21, 23, 25